HOW TO BE AN ANTIRACIST

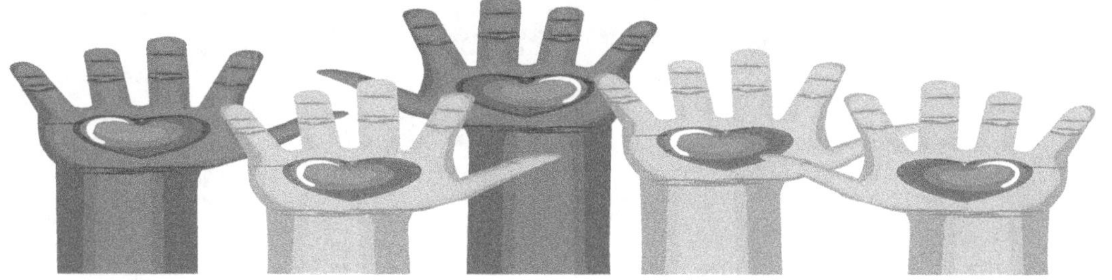

Note for parents,

For younger children it would be wonderful if you can help them to read the words and explain what they mean. Use the opportunity to discuss what the statements are trying to say, and how your child feels about them.

TATUS BRINAL

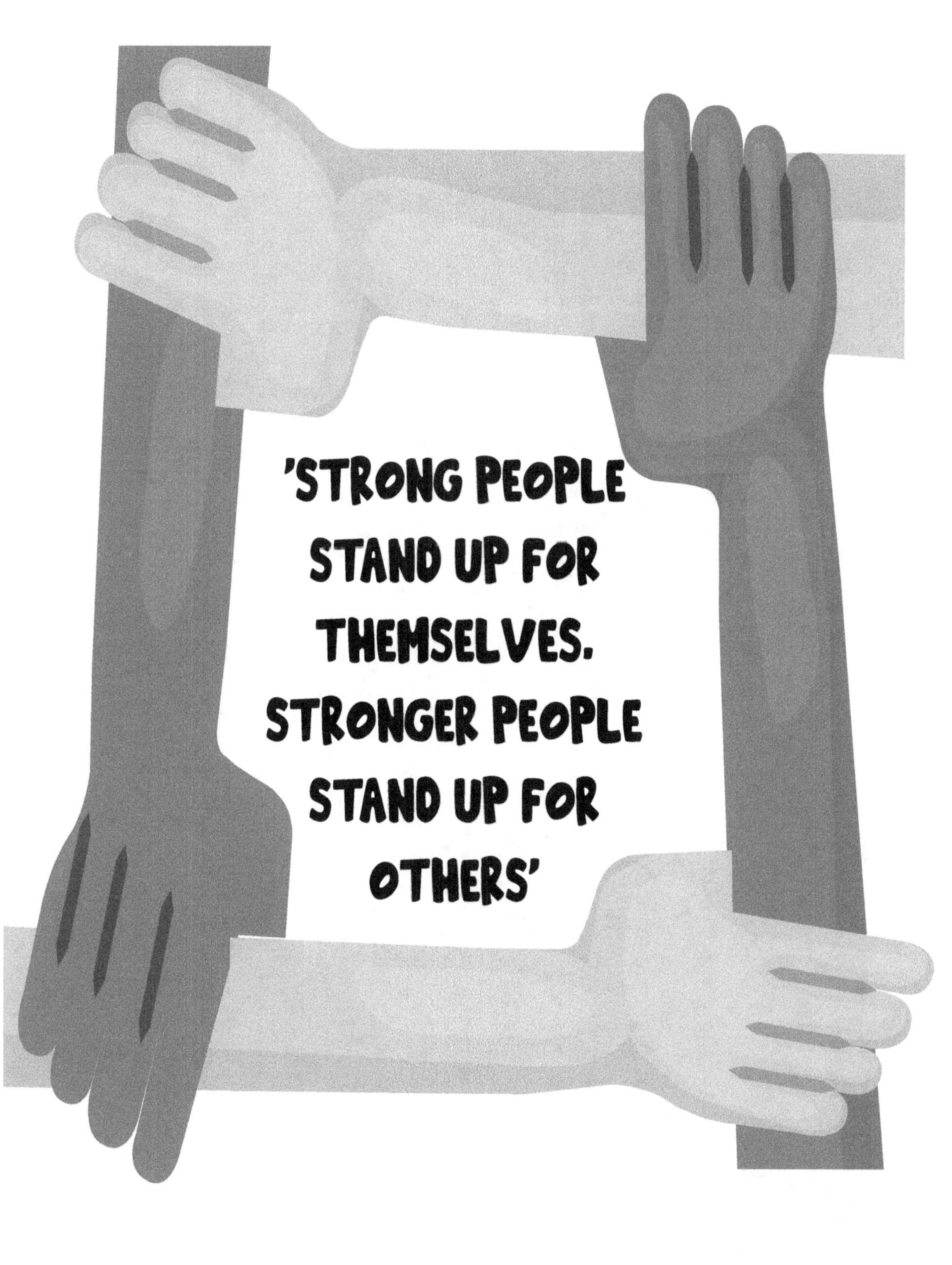

'STRONG PEOPLE STAND UP FOR THEMSELVES. STRONGER PEOPLE STAND UP FOR OTHERS'

IGNORANCE IS
STUBBORN
AND
PREJUDICE
IS HARD.

JUSTICE
IS
TRUTH
IN
ACTION

BEAUTY HAS
NO
SKIN TONE

AN EYE FOR
AN EYE MAKES
THE WHOLE
WORLD BLIND.

I DESTROY MY ENEMIES WHEN I MAKE THEM MY FRIENDS.

YOU CANNOT CHANGE WHAT PEOPLE SAY, BUT YOU CAN CHANGE HOW YOU REACT

THE ONLY
THING THAT
SHOULD
BE SEPARATED
BY COLOR
IS LANDRY

IF YOU WANT PEACE, WORK FOR JUSTICE.

IF YOU WANT TO MAKE PEACE, YOU DON'T TALK TO YOUR FRIENDS. YOU TALK TO YOUR ENEMIES.

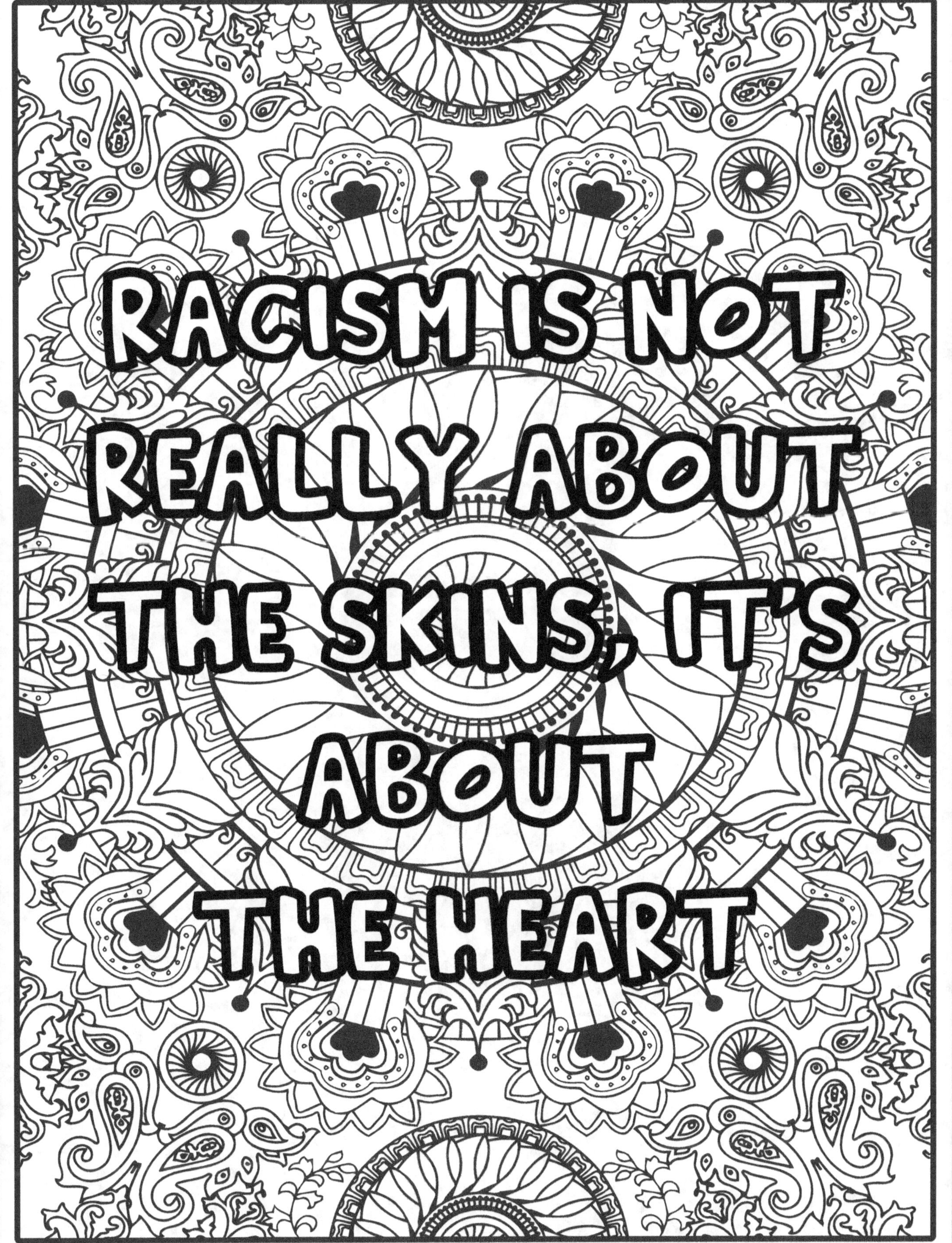

RACISM IS NOT REALLY ABOUT THE SKINS, IT'S ABOUT THE HEART

IDEOLOGIES SEPARATE US DREAMS AND ANGUISH BRING US TOGETHER.

INJUSTICE ANYWHERE IS A THREAT TO JUSTICE EVERYWHERE.

PEOPLE ONLY SEE WHAT THEY ARE PREPARED TO SEE

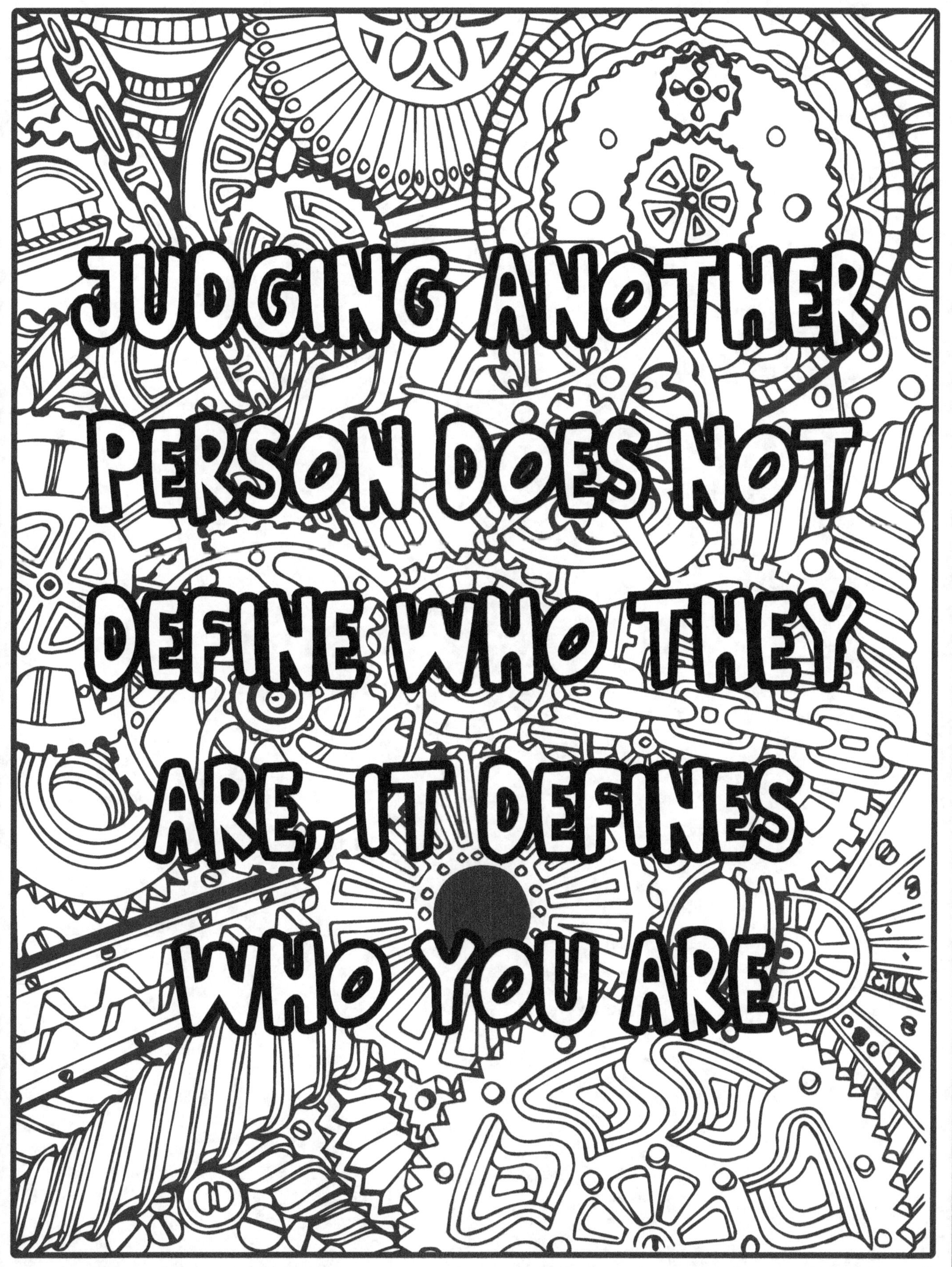

JUDGING ANOTHER PERSON DOES NOT DEFINE WHO THEY ARE, IT DEFINES WHO YOU ARE

IT IS NEVER
TOO LATE
TO GIVE UP
YOUR
PREJUDICES

NO FUTURE
WITHOUT
FORGIVENESS

PREJUDICE IS
AN OPINION
WITHOUT
JUDGMENT

THE TIME IS
ALWAYS RIGHT
TO DO WHAT
IS RIGHT

RACIAL
SUPERIORITY
IS A
MERE PIGMENT
OF THE
IMAGINATION

PREJUDICES
ARE THE
PROPS OF
CIVILIZATION

THE VERY INK WITH WHICH ALL HISTORY IS WRITTEN IS MERELY FLUID PREJUDICE

TO KNOW WHAT IS RIGHT AND NOT TO DO IT IS THE WORST COWARDICE

THE BEST WAY
TO FIND
YOURSELF IS
TO LOSE
YOURSELF IN THE
SERVICE
OF OTHERS

TO BE NEGRO
IN AMERICA
IS TO HOPE
AGAINST
HOPE

SEEING
IS NOT
ALWAYS
BELIEVING

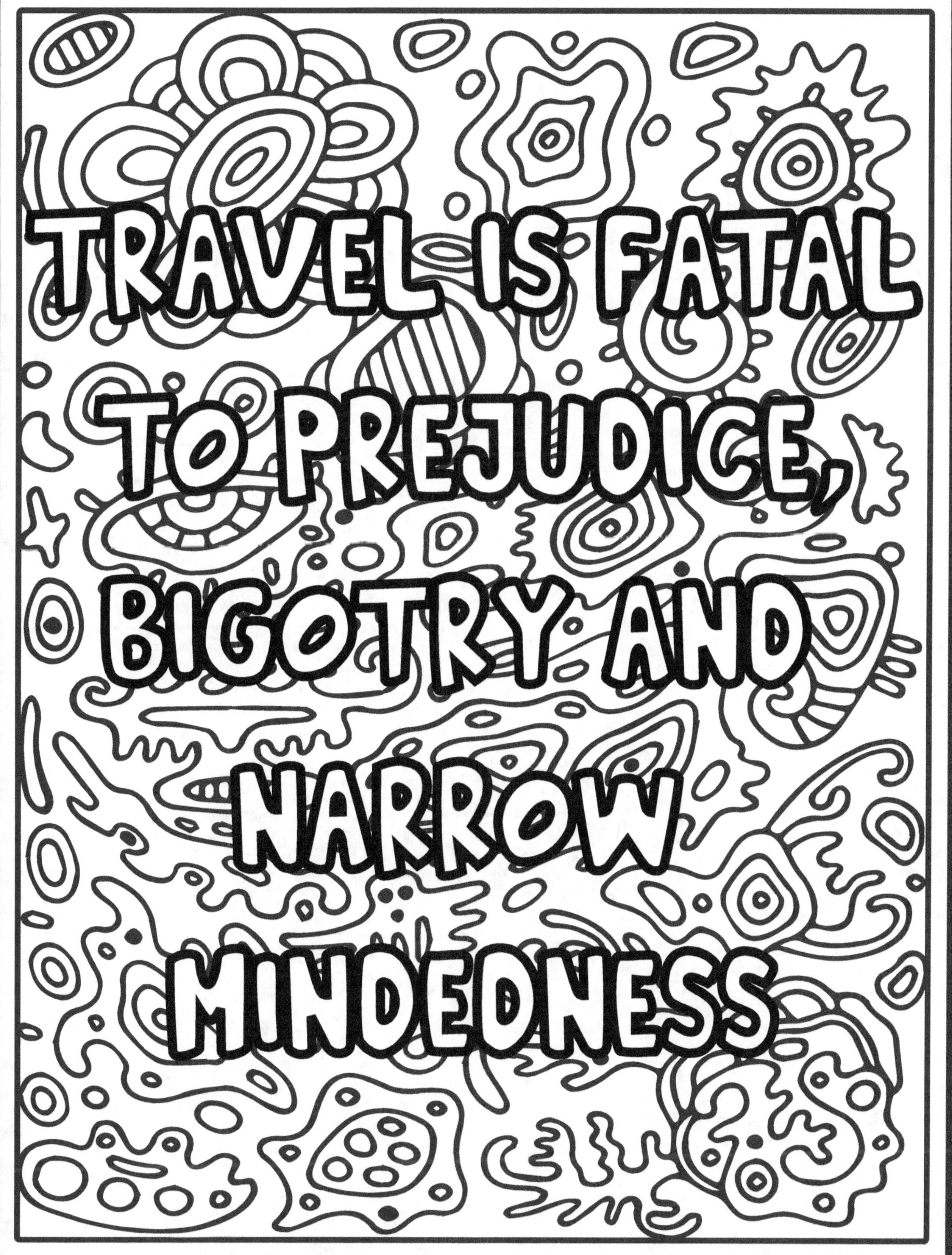

TRAVEL IS FATAL
TO PREJUDICE,
BIGOTRY AND
NARROW
MINDEDNESS

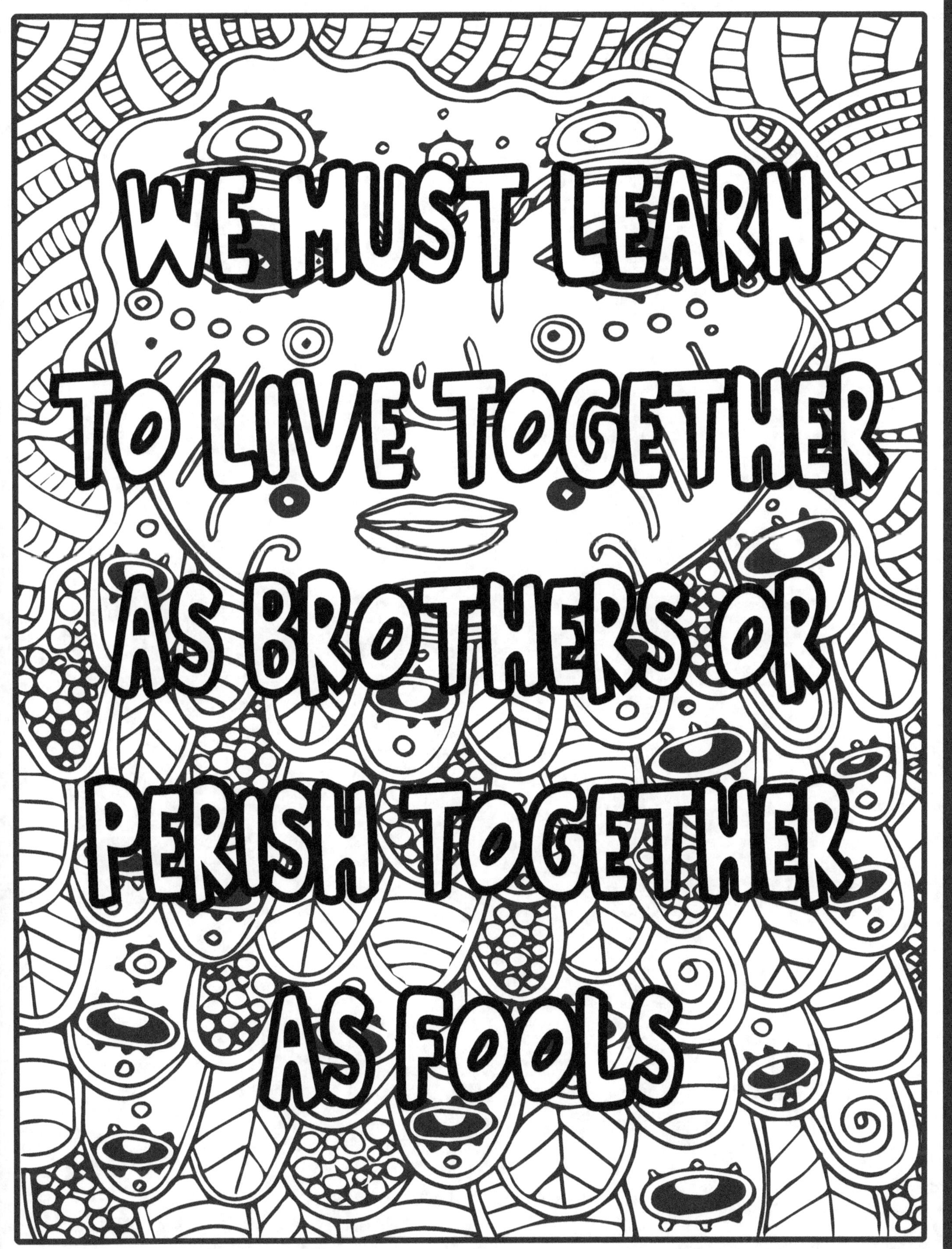

WE MUST LEARN
TO LIVE TOGETHER
AS BROTHERS OR
PERISH TOGETHER
AS FOOLS

VIOLENCE WILL ONLY INCREASE THE CYCLE OF VIOLENCE

WE ALL DECRY PREJUDICE,
YET ARE ALL PREJUDICED

WE MUST BE THE CHANGE WE WISH TO SEE IN THE WORLD